BARCELONA
style

To Alma

Published in 2025 by Welbeck
An Imprint of HEADLINE PUBLISHING GROUP LIMITED

1

Cataloguing in Publication Data is available from the British Library

ISBN 9781035423774

Printed and bound in China

Headline's policy is to use papers that are natural, renewable and recyclable products and made from wood grown in well-managed forests and other controlled sources. The logging and manufacturing processes are expected to conform to the environmental regulations of the country of origin.

HEADLINE PUBLISHING GROUP LIMITED
An Hachette UK Company
Carmelite House
50 Victoria Embankment
London EC4Y 0DZ

The authorized representative in the EEA is Hachette Ireland, 8 Castlecourt Centre, Dublin 15, D15 XTP3, Ireland (email: info@hbgi.ie)

www.headline.co.uk
www.hachette.co.uk

LAIA FARRAN GRAVES

BARCELONA style

CONTENTS

INTRODUCTION

"Barcelona is a very old city in which you can feel the weight of history; it is haunted by history. You cannot walk around it without perceiving it."
Carlos Ruiz Zafón

Barcelona is one of the most inspiring and stylish cities in the world, a place where you can easily lose yourself. You cannot truly appreciate its fashion without considering the city's architecture, landscape, culture, history, music and food – every facet of this extraordinary place comes together to create a unique identity and style that can be seen nowhere else.

From a bird's-eye view this magical city looks like a flawless grid, with a perfectly symmetrical pattern, devised in the nineteenth century by the urban planner and civil engineer Ildefons Cerdà. It sweeps down from the Collserola mountain range to the Mediterranean Sea, with a port and the hill of Montjuïc on one side and long beaches on the other. In this ideal location Barcelona has become a perfect representative of the Mediterranean lifestyle, with its relaxed approach to life, strong community values and unique creative flair.

Rosalía on stage in Madrid during
the Motomami tour in 2022.

Barcelona's story begins in the old city, nestled behind the port. Here you will find Roman remains and beautiful medieval buildings like the Cathedral and the fourteenth-century Santa Maria del Mar, amid squares, arches and narrow cobbled streets. Shaped by its history, Barcelona, now the capital of the autonomous community of Catalonia, has inherited a rich cultural legacy steeped in tradition, but is also innovative and visionary. This has resulted in incredible movements such as Catalan Modernism, whose greatest exponent was the architect Antoni Gaudí, responsible for the Sagrada Família and the Parc Güell. Other extraordinary artists include Joan Miró, Antoni Tàpies and Picasso (who spent nine years of his youth in Barcelona and remained closely connected to the city – his first name "Pablo" is "Pau" in Catalan); musicians such as Montserrat Caballé (who famously sang the hit 'Barcelona' with Freddie Mercury), cellist and composer Pau Casals, jazz pianist Tete Montoliu and, more recently, pop and style icon Rosalía; as well as chefs like Ferran Adrià and sports personalities including ex-player and football manager Pep Guardiola and Grand Prix motorcycle champion Marc Márquez.

Theatre, opera, cinema and dance are also very prominent, with companies like La Fura dels Baus, founded in 1979, known for their unusual urban locations and described by *NME* as an "adult adventure playground of fun, danger, slapstick and fantasy"); the legendary comedy trio Tricicle (created in 1979); and spectacular venues like El Palau de la Música Catalana (built between 1905 and 1908 by architect Lluís Domènech i Montaner), L'Auditori (designed in 1999 by Rafael Moneo) and the famous opera house, El Gran Teatre del Liceu (first opened in its present location

The Palace of Catalan Music (Palau de la Música Catalana) was built in 1908 by architect Domènech i Montaner. Its interior features beautiful stained-glass windows.

in 1847, redesigned by Josep Oriol Mestres i Esplugas in 1862 after a fire, and by Ignasi de Solà-Morales after another fire in 1999). There is also an abundance of museums in Barcelona, from the Museu Nacional d'Art de Catalunya (MNAC), with its overview of Catalan art through the centuries, to the many exciting modern art galleries all over the city.

Alongside the famous human castles, the *castellers*, Barcelona also enjoys a traditional Catalan dance, the *sardana*, which follows a sequence of steps performed in a circle. Dancers hold hands representing harmony, equality and liberty to the tunes of a small street band called the *cobla*. Although it can be danced impromptu at any street celebration, the traditional dress code for the participants includes the espadrille, or *espardenya*. Today, this humble shoe is very much coveted and can be found in its purest form at La Manual Alpargatera, the first espadrille store founded in Barcelona in 1940. It began as a small workshop and its celebrity clients include Jack Nicholson, Michael Douglas, Catherine Zeta-Jones and Julianne Moore.

Above: Traditional espadrilles in all colours and patterns at La Manual Alpargatera.

Opposite: Traditional espadrilles are part of the local Catalan costume.

Under Franco's dictatorship (1939–75), Catalan – the Romance language spoken in Catalonia – was repressed, forcing many into exile. Today, it remains Barcelona's official language and is dominant in all Catalonian schools. Catalan literature has also played an important role in revitalizing Catalan identity, especially since the end of the nineteenth century.

The cosmopolitan city is, of course, also a fashion hub and home to many global influencers, and celebrates its own fashion week, 080 Barcelona Fashion. It takes place in the Recinte Modernista de Sant Pau – one of the many wonderful buildings gracing the city. Among the brands founded in the city, or that have found their home there, are Mango, Tous, Desigual, Alohas, Massimo Dutti, Custo Barcelona, Pronovias and Paloma Wool, ranging from high street stalwarts to bespoke bridal.

Having the perfect weather also lends itself to enjoying many outside activities: every year Barcelona hosts an array of music festivals that have become internationally acclaimed, including Sónar, Primavera, Brunch Electronik and the renowned Barcelona Jazz Festival.

In 1992, Barcelona welcomed the rest of the world when it was selected to host the Games of the XXV Olympiad. The games transformed and modernized the city yet again, marking a new chapter and leaving an exemplary legacy that has promoted sport among its other attractions. Events such as the 2024 Barcelona Superyacht Regatta, a three-day racing event alongside Louis Vuitton's 37th America's Cup, can now take place at the Olympic Port.

Image from the *Mango Story Of Uniqueness* campaign for Spring/Summer 2017. The Catalan brand has achieved international success.

Catalonia's typical cuisine is another example of Barcelona's simple yet sublime pleasures. One of its local markets, the Mercat de Sant Josep (popularly known as La Boqueria), on the picturesque La Rambla (also known as Les Rambles) – the wide pedestrian mall leading to the port – has become one of the city's best-known landmarks. Bursting with colour and flavour, it is frequented by locals and travellers alike. Delicious traditional dishes, which you will find in many small restaurants and local *cafeterias*, include *pa amb tomàquet* (bread rubbed with tomato and seasoned with olive oil and salt), *escalivada* (roasted aubergine, tomatoes and red pepper with olive oil, garlic and spring onion), *botifarra negra amb mongeta blanca* (Catalan black sausage with white broad beans) and *crema catalana* – a dessert similar to *crème brûlée* flavoured with citrus and cinnamon and served with a caramelized sugar crust, and the perfect accompaniment to a strong cup of coffee.

This is a snapshot of what Barcelona has to offer: a stylish and cosmopolitan city that is host to chic residents – both permanent and visiting – who seek sun, sea, style, music, food and drink in a beautiful and storied setting.

Above: A chalkboard menu from the Mercat de Santa Caterina, located in the heart of the city.

Opposite: The “Created in Barcelona” sign featured at Primavera Sound in 2018, the music festival that took place at the Parc del Fòrum in Barcelona.

chapter 1

CATALAN ICONS

LEGENDARY CATALANS

"Allow me to state here how much I love Barcelona, an admirable city, a city full of life, intense, a port open to the past and future."

Le Corbusier

Across disciplines and throughout the decades, here are some of Catalonia's most influential, fascinating and talented personalities, all of whom have made their mark in history – and on the style DNA of the region and its capital.

From bestselling and world-famous musicians, pop stars and sports stars to globally acclaimed architects who have shaped the city's skyscape, and artists whose work you can see in the fantastic museums and art galleries in the city – most notably the Museu Nacional d'Art de Catalunya (MNAC), the Fundació Antoni Tàpies, the Museu Picasso, the Museu d'Art Contemporani (MACBA), the Fundació Joan Miró, the Centre de Cultura Contemporània de Barcelona (CCCB) and CaixaForum. These cultural centres form the backbone of Barcelona's visual identity, with each style and aesthetic reflecting an individual creative vision.

Surrealist artist Salvador Dalí was as iconic sartorially as he was culturally.

ART

Antoni Gaudí (1852–1926)

Described by many as a genius, the internationally acclaimed Catalan architect Antoni Gaudí (1852–1926) has become known for his unique and distinct flamboyant style. He was part of Catalonia's Modernisme movement, and his work is characterized by the use of dynamic and organic shapes, often utilizing curves and striking decorative ornaments and finishes such as his kaleidoscopic mosaic tiling.

"Originality consists of going back to the origins."
Antoni Gaudí

This form of architectural expression, which emerged at the end of the nineteenth century and is connected to Art Nouveau, extended into other cultural fields such as art and literature. Led by bohemians and intellectuals, the Modernists used the arts to distance themselves from some of the traditional and bourgeois values of the time, reinforcing a Catalan national identity and an attitude that resonates through the style and culture of the region to this day.

The spectacular Casa Batlló was designed by the modernist Catalan architect Antoni Gaudí.

Louis Vuitton paid homage to Antoni Gaudí
for the Cruise 2025 collection.

Gaudí was born on 25 June 1852, near Reus, in the province of Tarragona, into a family of coppersmiths. As a young child, his health was poor, so he spent a lot of time resting and observing the wonders of nature. This would have a huge influence on his work in later life and become a constant source of inspiration. He loved to go on long walks, and, unusually (and on the advice of his physician), he was a vegetarian.

In 1870 he moved to Barcelona to study architecture. When he graduated in 1878, Elies Rogent, the school director, remarked: "I do not know if we have awarded this degree to a madman or to a genius; only time will tell." That same year, he exhibited his work at the Exposition Universelle in Paris, where he met the illustrious politician and businessman Eusebi Güell (1846–1918). On seeing Gaudí's exhibit, Güell had insisted that he wanted to meet the designer. Later, he became his patron.

When designing, Gaudí rarely sketched plans; instead, he worked from 3D models of his future constructions – a brilliant, unorthodox technique that added to his naturalist, fluid trademark. He was also known for being inventive and is said to have started his characteristic mosaic work, the *trencadís* style, because a tile order he had placed arrived broken, and he had no time to wait for a new replacement shipment.

Some of Gaudí's most notable masterpieces, which have had a significant impact on the Catalan architectural landscape and beyond, include the Torre Bellesguard; Parc Güell; the restoration of the Catedral de Mallorca; the church on the Güell estate; Casa Batlló; Casa Milà; and the imposing church of the Sagrada Família – perhaps his most magnificent creation and certainly the most well-known. These works have been described by the UNESCO Foundation as exceptional and outstanding contributions to our architectural heritage, and are now listed as UNESCO World Heritage Sites.

Gaudí's final years were primarily devoted to his work on the Sagrada Família; he took over the project in 1883, and never saw it finished. He became utterly absorbed in this masterpiece and the project prompted him to take a more spiritual path in his personal life, leaving behind his previous, more sociable persona. In 1926, just before his 74th birthday, he was hit by a tram on his way to a church where he used to go and pray. Apparently he didn't hear its whistle and because he liked to wear simple, frayed clothes, passers-by took him for a beggar and didn't recognize him. He later died in hospital of his injuries. Huge crowds followed his funeral procession to the Sagrada Família where he was buried, and years later, in 2010, his beloved holy temple was consecrated by Pope Benedict XVI.

His legacy has motivated many fashion designers over time. For instance, Hervé Léger by Max Azria's Autumn/Winter 2015 collection, shown at New York Fashion Week, was inspired by the Sagrada Família, using the architect's symbolism to express nativity, passion and glory. In 2024, an exhibition called *Bajo la influencia de Gaudí* ("Under Gaudí's influence"), organized by the Fashion Art Institute and by designer Manuel Fernández, brought together collaborations from 19 creatives, each representing a different autonomous community in Spain, which explored the fusion between art, fashion and architecture; and in 2024, Louis Vuitton's Nicolas Ghesquière paid homage to the architect by presenting the 2025 Cruise Collection at Parc Güell, in a timeless classic show that seemed to meld perfectly with its surroundings.

The architecture of Antoni Gaudí inspired Hervé Léger by Max Azria's A/W 2015 Ready-to-Wear collection.

Salvador Dalí (1904–89)

Salvador Dalí is regarded as one of the most accomplished and versatile Surrealist painters of all time. Born in Figueres in 1904, he became known for his flamboyant personality, his hyperrealistic style, and for using shocking images in his work. His best-known painting is perhaps *The Persistence of Memory* (1931), which depicts a series of melting clocks, all showing different times, in a deserted landscape. His artistic repertoire is exceptionally versatile and ranges from sculpture, printmaking, fashion, advertising and writing to filmmaking (collaborating with Luis Buñuel, Walt Disney and Alfred Hitchcock). He also wrote several texts, including his autobiography, *The Secret Life of Salvador Dalí,* published in 1942.

"A true artist is not one who is inspired, but one who inspires others."
Salvador Dalí

Aware of his talent and exceptional technical skill, his parents sent him to art school in 1916 and soon after he had his first exhibition. In 1922 Dalí went on to study art at the Real Academia de Bellas Artes de San Fernando in Madrid, where he became familiar with classic painters such as Diego Velázquez – whose moustache he later adopted – and explored many art movements, including Cubism and Dadaism, eventually joining the Surrealist movement alongside Joan Miró and René Magritte.

The surrealist Salvador Dalí photographed in Cadaqués Port Lligat.

He made two films with director Luis Buñuel: *Un Chien Andalou* (*An Andalusian Dog*) in 1929 and *L'Âge d'Or* (*The Golden Age*) in 1930. At the presentation of his first film, he was introduced to the French poet Paul Éluard (one of the founders of the Surrealist art movement) and his future wife, Gala (Elena Ivanovna Diakonova). She became his muse and business manager.

During the Spanish Civil War (1936–39), Dalí and Gala lived in Paris. They moved to the United States in 1940 and returned to Spain in 1948.

Salvador Dalí became very much a part of the French art and fashion scenes. In September 1938, Coco Chanel invited him to La Pausa, her home on the French Riviera. He created various paintings there and later exhibited them at the Julien Levy Gallery in New York. He had a great interest in fashion and collaborated with the Italian designer Elsa Schiaparelli, working together on some of her most iconic designs, including the shoe hat and lobster dress. Schiaparelli reinterpreted his work through her tear and skeleton dresses, too, while Dalí created designs for her fragrance bottles. This partnership of iconoclasts resulted in some of the most experimental fashion of the twentieth century. Dalí's own personal style was as much a part of his Surrealist identity as his art – whether in a bold double-breasted pinstripe suit, traditional Catalan clothing or an ostentatiously frilled shirt. He always accessorized it with his instantly recognizable moustache, a gallant artistic statement.

The iconic Lobster dress was designed in 1937 by Elsa Schiaparelli and Salvador Dalí.

In 1948, Dalí and Gala moved back into their Catalan home – a house in Port Lligat, on the coast near Cadaqués, which became their base. He also travelled regularly to Paris and New York, reflecting his busy life and rising fame. Dalí died in 1989, and is buried in the crypt below the theatre in Figueres where his first exhibition took place. It is now the Teatre-Museu Dalí, the Dalí Theatre-Museum.

Joan Miró (1893–1983)

One of the world's most celebrated Catalan artists of the twentieth century, Miró is known for his paintings, ceramics, printmaking, collage, muralism, tapestry engraving and sculptures. His Surrealist, naive work has inspired, moved and influenced many, and some of his artwork – sculptures, tapestries and murals – can be seen in the heart of Barcelona itself. He donated four works of art to the city, strategically placed to welcome those arriving by air, sea or land. At Terminal 2 in Barcelona Airport, you will find the contrasting ceramic *Mural de l'Aeroport* (10m/33ft high and 50m/165 ft long). Halfway down La Rambla, located in Pla de l'Os, is a circular mosaic by Miró in vivid primary colours, displayed on the ground. The *Dona i ocell* statue (*Woman and Bird*), which is 22m (72ft) high, can be seen in the recently renamed and redesigned Parc de Joan Miró; and finally, you can visit the Fundació Joan Miró, created in 1975, one of Barcelona's best-known museums. This was Miró's last gift to the city: it sits on the hill of Montjuïc and is home to over 14,000 works of art.

The striking *Dona i ocell* (*Woman and Bird*) sculpture is located in Barcelona's Joan Miró park.

"For me, an object is a living thing."
Joan Miró

Born in Barcelona in 1893, Miró attended the Llotja Escola Superior d'Art i Disseny until 1910, while also taking a business studies course at the Escola de Comerç de Barcelona at his father's request. He then worked as a clerk for two years, but left the job due to illness and decided to dedicate his life to art. He studied at Francesc Galí's Escola d'Art in Barcelona from 1912 to 1915, where he was exposed to other European artists.

He first visited Paris in 1920 and met Pablo Picasso, Pierre Reverdy, Max Jacob, André Masson and Tristan Tzara. This was an exciting time in the art world, and Miró became part of a community of artists, many of whom travelled to the French capital during the early twentieth century and were known as the School of Paris. In 1929, Miró married Pilar Juncosa. They had a daughter and lived in Paris but travelled back to Spain regularly.

They spent the Spanish Civil War (1936–1939) in Paris and on the outbreak of the Second World War (1939–1945), Miró's friend, the architect George Nelson, offered him and his family a house on the Normandy coast, away from the city, where he later rented a property. This is where he started to paint a series of works which were later called *Constellations* – a series of 23 paintings on paper considered widely to be one of his career's greatest achievements. After much travelling, he eventually settled in Majorca in 1956, where his friend and acclaimed architect Josep Lluís Sert designed his beloved studio, the Taller Sert.

Joan Miró presented his work at the Marlborough Fine Art Galleries in London for his solo exhibition in May 1966.

After the war, his work rose to international fame and was exhibited worldwide. His first major retrospective was in 1941 in the Museum of Modern Art, New York. Joan Miró received many accolades during his career, including the Grand Prize for Graphic Work at the Venice Biennale in 1954. A year later, the first Documenta exhibition in Kassel included some of his pieces. He was also granted the Guggenheim International Award for his murals in the UNESCO building in Paris in 1958.

Above: Michael van der Ham's S/S 2013 collection references the art of Joan Miró.

Opposite: Inspired by Joan Miró, Diane von Furstenberg featured a red circle on a black dress in her A/W 2007 show.

Fashion and textile designers have long been inspired by his unconventional and playful use of shape and colour. Miró himself designed the cover of a Balenciaga exhibition catalogue, and guest-edited the December 1979 issue of *Vogue Paris*. Karl Lagerfeld borrowed his palette of bold colours for his Spring/Summer 2005 collection for Fendi; Diane von Furstenberg featured a red circle on a black dress in a nod to Miró for her Autumn/Winter 2007 show, and designer Michael van der Ham's Spring/Summer 2013 collection referenced the artist's work through painterly prints.

Karl Lagerfeld adopted Joan Miró's colours in his 2005 show for Fendi in Milan, Italy.

Antoni Tàpies (1923–2012)

The internationally acclaimed Antoni Tàpies is one of Barcelona's most important Surrealist artists, who went on to develop an abstract style. His work has been exhibited at the world's most important museums, including the Museum of Modern Art and the Solomon R. Guggenheim Museum in New York, the Institute of Contemporary Art and the Serpentine and Hayward Galleries in London, the Centre Pompidou in Paris and the MACBA in Barcelona.

Tàpies started painting when he was 17 while recovering from a serious illness. In 1943, after three years studying law at the University of Barcelona, he left to focus on his art and to exhibit his work.

Mostly self-taught, he co-founded the Dau al Set (Seven-sided dice), a group of artists, poets and philosophers with whom he published an artistic-literary review until 1953.

"Art should startle the viewer into thinking about the meaning of life."
Antoni Tàpies

The work of Jean Dubuffet in 1950 influenced him greatly and marked a turning point in his artistic career, indicating a departure from Surrealism to Abstract art. His work became experimental, and he used very textured canvases and impasto. He later added objects to his pieces, including buckets, mirrors and silk stockings as a means of expression.

It was an idea he took to the extreme in his assemblage *Desk and Straw* (1970), where he used a desk as his canvas. He also explored colour and geometrical shapes, for which he became well-known internationally.

Tàpies designed many lithographs and used some to illustrate books with the poet Joan Brossa. He also wrote a number of essays on art, politics and life which have been collected and published.

In 1984 he created the Fundació Antoni Tàpies to facilitate and promote modern and contemporary art. This cultural centre and museum, home to the largest collections of his work, is located in Barcelona's central Carrer d'Aragó, and holds regular exhibitions of his work, as well as lectures, film seasons and other activities. Here one can appreciate the huge influence of his work on Barcelona's artists and designers.

In 1990, Tàpies received the international arts prize Praemium Imperiale awarded by the Japan Art Association and in 2010, he was also awarded the hereditary title *marquès de Tàpies*.

Elsewhere, artists such as Claudy Jongstra, who creates artworks with strong social and environmental messages, specializing in tapestries and textile art installations, have also been greatly inspired by the works of Tàpies. Jongstra collaborated with Viktor&Rolf for their haute couture Autumn/Winter 2019 collection, and was commissioned by John Galliano to create a custom textile from felted wool on silk organza featured in the Maison Margiela Autumn/Winter 2018 couture artisanal collection. She also made a series of window installations for Hermès in Palermo called "Sheep to Wool".

The Catalan contemporary painter, sculptor and art theorist Antoni Tàpies, whose work influenced many.

MUSIC

Montserrat Caballé (1933–2018)

The unrivalled Montserrat Caballé, who was known as *La Superba* for her prodigious and unequalled voice, is regarded as one of the best sopranos in the world. Her fun and larger-than-life personality is beautifully reflected in her varied career, which spanned over six decades and earned her several tributes, including three Grammy Awards.

A child of the Spanish Civil War, Montserrat Caballé had a modest upbringing. She developed a love for singing from a young age, and in 1942, she received a scholarship to study at Barcelona's Conservatori Superior de Música del Liceu. After graduating with a gold medal, Montserrat moved to Basel in Switzerland and made her professional debut there in 1956. She sang with the Basel Opera Company between 1957 and 1959. In 1962, she debuted in Barcelona's Gran Teatre del Liceu; the following year, she toured Mexico.

Montserrat married the tenor Bernabé Martí (1928–2022) in 1964. The following year, she went down in history when she replaced Marilyn Horne, who was pregnant at the time, in Gaetano Donizetti's opera *Lucrezia Borgia* at Carnegie Hall in New York. Her outstanding performance resulted in a 25-minute ovation from the audience.

It was a turning point in her musical career, which led to debuts in the most established theatres, including the Metropolitan Opera, the Royal Opera House, the Vienna State Opera, the Glyndebourne Festival Opera, the Arena di Verona, the Lyric Opera of Chicago and the San Francisco Opera.

“When he sat down at the piano to improvise, I realized that a true musician was before me.”

Montserrat Caballé talking to EL PAÍS about Freddie Mercury

Freddie Mercury kisses opera singer Montserrat Caballé on the hand as they perform ‘Barcelona’ at a music festival in the city to celebrate the arrival of the Olympic flag from Seoul, 11 October 1988.

Caballé is also known for 'Barcelona', the duet she sang with Freddie Mercury – one of the most exciting musical collaborations of all time. She was asked to produce a theme song for the Olympics and approached Freddie Mercury, whom she had recently met. The song became one of Mercury's greatest hits as a solo artist, and was unique because it successfully brought together classical opera and rock music. Released in 1987, it reached number eight in the UK Singles Chart. Sadly, Mercury died before the 1992 Barcelona Olympics, when the song was again a huge success, reaching number two in the UK, the Netherlands and in New Zealand.

It was Montserrat Caballé who, in 1970, first noticed the voice of José Carreras in one of her own productions. She offered him his first adult role as a tenor in 1971 – he made his international debut in London's Festival Hall, in *Maria Stuarda*, with Caballé in the title role – and went on to help him establish his career for many years. Known for being one of the famous Three Tenors, Carreras is another outstanding musician from Barcelona.

Caballé's fabulous style, both on and off stage, were all part of her prima donna identity – though privately she was a very down-to-earth person who was devoted to her family. A seamstress from Barcelona made her iconic gowns and she herself would style her own jet-black hair and dramatic makeup. Since her death, her famous operatic costumes have been exhibited online and at the Palau Güell. Those heavily embellished gowns in silk, brocade and chiffon covered in rhinestones and embroidery with dramatic sleeves and shoulders have all contributed to her iconic *diva* look.

The extraordinary Montserrat Caballé is considered one of the greatest soprano singers of her time.

Rosalía

The Catalan singer and songwriter Rosalía Vila i Tobella (b 1992), known simply as Rosalía, has taken the music world by storm. She has redefined it by creating her own genre – putting her stamp on flamenco-inspired music by fusing it with hip-hop and other influences.

She rose to fame in 2018 with her single 'Malamente', which resulted in five Latin Grammy Award nominations and an MTV Europe Music Awards gig. The following year, her collaboration with Colombian rapper J Balvin on 'Con Altura' produced the most-watched music video by a female artist on YouTube that year, reaching billions. Rosalía has also appeared in the Oscar-nominated film *Dolor y gloria* (*Pain and Glory*), starring Antonio Banderas and Penélope Cruz, directed by the legendary Pedro Almodóvar.

Rosalía started singing as a child and immersed herself in the world of flamenco by listening to it and learning its dance, then studied it formally at the Taller de Músics in Barcelona, which accepts only one student per year to its flamenco program. In 2017 she graduated from the Escola Superior de Música de Catalunya and that same year released her first album, *Los Ángeles*, as part of her graduate thesis.

Rosalía has become a feminist icon in her quest to break down gender barriers, and often surrounds herself with women in her shows and videos. An example of this is her bestselling album *Motomami*, launched in 2022, which she defines as an energy – being resourceful and doing what you

Rosalía attends the 'Prelude to the Olympics' at the Fondation Louis Vuitton in Paris in 2024.

Her ability to mix musical styles has seen the pop and flamenco singer Rosalía described as an “atypical pop star”.

can with what you have. Rosalia wishes the album, which has been described as an avant-garde feminist manifesto and features many female contributors, "provides a feminist counterbalance to misogyny in music". A major fashion influence, she has starred in campaigns for Acne Studios and Skims, and performed at Louis Vuitton's Autumn/Winter 2023 show. She has featured on the red carpet at the Met Gala several times, appearing in 2021 in a showstopping Rick Owens red leather design inspired by the *mantón de Manila* fringed scarf. Off-duty, now living in Florida, her fun and eclectic personal style is in keeping with her Barcelona roots. She's as likely to sport a moto jacket and shield glasses as she is to wear baggy trousers and a crop top – often wearing fiery red shades or flowing ruffles that reference flamenco style.

"Barcelona is an open and multicultural city. It's brimming with a very special creative energy. If you pay attention, you may be easily inspired by the places and people living there."
Rosalía

During her career she has received many awards and nominations, including four MTV Video Music Awards, an MTV Europe Music Award, two Grammy Awards and 12 Latin Grammy Awards, including the 2019 and 2022 Grammy Award for best Latin Rock, Urban or Alternative Album. This makes her the first woman to win Album of the Year twice.

CUISINE

Food is central to Barcelona, and eating in style is an absolute must. In the fast-paced world we live in, most stores and many businesses, especially the most traditional, still close at lunchtime and resume business at 5pm, allowing time for an enjoyable lunch. When eating, the table is always laid beautifully, and it is customary at lunch and dinner to enjoy an entry dish, a main course and a dessert. Catalan cuisine is sophisticated and complex, with many traditional recipes being passed down through generations. It also enjoys exquisite wines and cava, also known as Catalan champagne, from local vineyards, which has been a hugely successful export.

Ferran Adrià

Catalan chef Ferran Adrià is best known for breaking barriers in the food industry and for creating the concept of molecular gastronomy, using science to create experiential haute cuisine. Such has been his global influence that in 2004 he was included in *Time* magazine's list of 100 Most Innovative People.

Born in 1962, Ferran grew up in Barcelona and left his studies to wash dishes in the restaurant at the Hotel Playafels – apparently in order to fund a stay in Ibiza. In 1982, when he did his compulsory military service (serving in the navy), he joined the admiral's kitchen for a year and ended up being in charge of it full time. There he met another budding chef, Fermí Puig, whom he befriended and who suggested that he tried working at El Bulli, a restaurant on the Costa Brava.

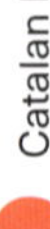

In 2004, Ferran Adrià was included in *Time* magazine's list of 100 Most Innovative People.

This he did during his month's leave in the summer of 1983, and the internship was a success. Following his military service, Adrià joined the team at the restaurant, kept his head down and worked his way up, while experimenting and being creative. By 1987 he was appointed the sole *chef de cuisine*.

His approach to cooking, both rigorous and experimental, set him apart from other chefs. He created new and unexpected sensations for his diners by applying scientific techniques. One example of this is what he called "spherification". By enveloping fluids with gelatine spheres, he made playful dishes such as liquid olives, which appear solid but burst with olive juice in the mouth.

"Eating well is something you can do at home. The point about what we offer is that it is more than eating; it is an experience."

Ferran Adrià

In 1990, he became co-owner of the restaurant, and by the end of the decade, his restaurant had received three Michelin Stars, the maximum that can be awarded. The restaurant received many awards, such as being voted the Best Restaurant in the World in 2002 by the British industry publication *Restaurant*, and again from 2006 to 2009.

Despite being one of the most coveted restaurants at the time, with long waiting lists and a huge demand, El Bulli closed down in 2011 to become the elBullifoundation, a non-profit foundation dedicated to culinary research. The restaurant, now called elBulli1846, reflecting the number of dishes created by the restaurant while it was open, is open to the public as a museum during the summer months.

But his creativity and his artistic expression don't stop there. His favourite fashion designer is the Catalan Antonio Miró, and he bought clothes from his shop, Groc, when it first opened. After 25 years of wearing white, Ferran now opts for black ensembles. His wife, Isabel Pérez Barcelo, is known for her elegance and loves many designers including Issey Miyake – a designer Ferran discovered and is a fan of himself.

SPORTS

Pep Guardiola

Josep Guardiola i Sala, known as Pep Guardiola, was born in the town of Santpedor near Barcelona, in 1971. He grew up as a Barcelona Football Club fan and loved the sport so much that he joined his local youth team, Club Gimnàstic de Manresa. A talented player, he was transferred to join the under-16 squad of the Barcelona Football Club aged 13.

In 1990, he joined the main squad (1990–2001) and became part of the Dream Team managed by Johan Cruyff, a former player himself. As a defensive midfielder for Barça, known as "the child of Santpedor", Guardiola scored 16 goals in his 479 appearances over 11 years. During 1991 and 1994, Barcelona FC won La Liga four consecutive times, the European Cup in 1992 and Olympic gold with Spain that same year. He was made team captain in 1997 and held this title until he left the club in 2001. He then played for several other teams before his retirement as a player, including Brescia and AS Roma in Italy and Dorados de Sinaloa in Mexico.

During his career as a footballer Guardiola won six La Liga titles, four Spanish Super Cup titles and the Copa del Rey twice, and in 1992 won Olympic gold with the Spanish national team as well as the UEFA European Football Championship. But he is perhaps better known as a football manager and is widely considered a tactical genius. He managed the Barcelona C and then the B teams before becoming Barcelona FC's manager from 2008 to 2012, with Lionel Messi as their star striker, making them treble winners – they won the domestic cup (the Copa del Rey), La Liga (the equivalent of the Premier League in England) and the UEFA Champions League in 2008/9. He was named the FIFA World Coach of the Year in 2011 after further victories. Pep then moved to Bayern Munich in 2013 and, in 2016, became Manchester City's coach.

Guardiola's influence in the sport goes beyond the matches he has competed in and coached: he has changed the way football is played, for instance, by involving the goalkeeper in the game itself and perfecting the smooth *tiquitaca* style of passing the ball to retain possession. As a manager, he holds the record for winning the most consecutive league games in La Liga, the Bundesliga and the Premier League, making him a true sporting legend.

Guardiola has become known for his personal style on the sidelines, often sporting a chunky rollneck or cardigan, or layered white T-shirt and dark crew neck knit – with a monochrome look that is more tech entrepreneur than football manager. In 2014, he married Cristina Serra, a Brazilian writer and stylist who also runs the Barcelona fashion boutique Serra Claret, a family business, with her sister Judith.

Ex-football player and manager Pep Guardiola has influenced the game of football globally.

chapter 2

CATALAN FASHiON

A FASHION DESTINATION

Barcelona's fashion industry began in the early twentieth century. The region had a prosperous textile industry and much prestige – French couture designer Jeanne Lanvin first trained with a dressmaker in Barcelona. In 1919 Pedro Rodríguez, originally from Valencia, opened his first haute couture store in Barcelona, which, following the guidelines of Parisian haute couture, showed a collection each season. Lanvin herself opened her Barcelona store in 1920 and, in 1929, couturier Cristóbal Balenciaga exhibited his work at the Exposició Internacional de Barcelona. During the 1940s, Rodríguez was one of the instigators of the Haute Couture Cooperative in Barcelona (alongside Manuel Pertegaz, Asunción Bastida, Santa Eulalia and El Dique Flotante), and served as president. They promoted the industry worldwide and dressed many aristocrats, Hollywood actresses and socialites.

Today, the city has become a popular shopping destination, which offers local and international designers in its many fashion districts, such as the Passeig de Gràcia or La Rambla. Some Catalan designers who have grown to enjoy global success include bridal gown firms, formal knitwear boutiques, streetwear brands, accessories, jewellery and even global fragrance companies.

A colourful poster for the International Exhibition in Barcelona 1929, which left a significant architectural legacy on the city.

EXPOSICIÓN
INTERNACIONAL
BARCELONA 1929

PRONOVIAS

In 1922, fleeing the First World War, street vendor Alberto Palatchi Bienveniste arrived in Barcelona from Turkey, carrying a suitcase full of embroidery. He opened a shop which he called El Suizo near the emblematic Plaça de Catalunya – Alberto was blond and had blue eyes and was known as the "the Swiss". The store specialized in selling lace, embroidery and silk to Catalan families to embellish their gowns for special occasions, as well as for bridal attire. It was later turned into a workshop that he named St. Patrick, which later became part of the Pronovias Group.

The brand grew in popularity. They were now designing and making dresses, and in 1964, the business took a groundbreaking new direction when they incorporated the concept of ready-to-wear into their traditional, exclusively bridal designs, creating complete collections. Four years later, they opened their first bridal fashion store in Barcelona, followed by 61 more boutiques in other Spanish cities in less than two years.

The business grew further, and in 1968, Pronovias launched its logo and staged its very first fashion show at the boutique in Barcelona's prestigious Passeig de Gràcia under the label St. Patrick. In 1969, Alberto's son – also called Alberto Palatchi – took over the company and was appointed general manager. Helped by his wife, businesswoman

A classic Pronovias piece on the runway at New York Bridal Fashion Week.

Above: A timeless modern classic from the Pronovias Fashion Show during Barcelona Bridal Week in 2024.

Overleaf: A stunning Pronovias collection was shown as part of the Barcelona Bridal Week in 2023.

Susana Gallardo, he modernized and revolutionized the brand, transforming Pronovias into one of the world's most prominent and largest wedding dress companies globally. An order was placed from Holland in 1980, which marked the start of their expansion across Europe, with stores soon opening in Germany, France, the United Kingdom and Italy.

"Craftsmanship and design intertwine in our Barcelona workshop, a unique creative haven where dreams are meticulously transformed into exquisite pieces of art, stitch by stitch."

Pronovias.com

The talented designer Manuel Mota (1966–2013) joined the house as creative director in 1990, a post he held until his unexpected early death. During the 1990s, he developed a new concept, Pronovias Costura (Pronovias Couture), first launched in their central Barcelona store (on the Via Augusta near Avinguda Diagonal). It elevated the brand by bringing together ready-to-wear clothing with couture. An atelier was also incorporated in 1994, drawing on their expertise to create exquisite bridal couture pieces.

In 2002, Pronovias opened its first flagship store in the heart of Paris, on rue Tronchet. Between 2003 and 2011, the maison went through a very creative period that is now described as the "era of collaborations", working with designers, including Lydia Delgado, Emanuel Ungaro, Valentino and Elie Saab.

New flagship stores opened internationally, in key cities such as London, New York, Dubai, Milan, Mexico and Tokyo, consolidating their global presence, and in 2017 Palatchi sold 90 per cent of Pronovias to the private British equity firm BC Partners for an estimated $550 million.

Like many luxury brands that have triumphed in the fashion world, Pronovias began as a small family business. Focusing on heritage, craftsmanship and attention to detail has ensured its success. Dresses are made by hand and can take up to 120 hours to complete, so that each bride feels unique and special on her big day. A collection created for special occasions, including garments for cocktail parties and red-carpet events is also available.

Today, Pronovias sells in 105 countries worldwide and has 123 stores with over 4,000 points of sale. Over 600 original dresses are designed yearly, making Barcelona the second-largest bridal market in the world – China being the first.

In 2024, to celebrate its 60th anniversary, Pronovias presented a collection showcasing architectural and minimal designs at Barcelona's Bridal Fashion Week. The show took place in the impressive MNAC (Museu Nacional d'Art de Catalunya) and reflected Barcelona's art and culture as the inspiration behind the Atelier Pronovias 2025 show. Not only did it raise the bar, it also marked a new era for the company, catering to modern, cosmopolitan women without leaving behind classic elegance and romance.

Beautiful colours were seen at the Escorpion fashion show at 080 Barcelona Fashion in 2023.

ESCORPION

Founded in 1929, Escorpion began as a women's knitwear company and established itself as a quiet, traditional, luxury brand using the simple strapline *Un jersey Escorpion* (an Escorpion sweater). The brand has adapted to emerging trends through the decades but has always been faithful to empowering strong, independent women.

During the 1970s, Escorpion opened its own stores. Escorpion currently sells garments in 900 stores worldwide in over 20 countries, and their collections are available in many independent boutiques and in the legendary department store El Corte Inglés all over Spain. Their commitment to sustainability is paramount, and when manufacturing their collections, they focus on quality, not quantity.

Since 2011, they have shown their collections at 080 Barcelona Fashion, and in 2015 they launched a diffusion line called Escorpion Studio Barcelona, a capsule collection targeted to a younger audience that combines elegance with creativity while honouring Escorpion's heritage.

Jessica Raya Ferrer is Escorpion's design director, responsible for some of their most successful 080 Barcelona Fashion shows. Un jersey Escorpion, the Autumn/Winter 2023 collection shown at the 32nd edition of Barcelona Fashion Week, was an ode to the brand or, as described in their press release, a reinterpretation of their DNA. Using earthy tones combined with azure, petal, rosewood and grey, it featured classic, elegant and sometimes asymmetrical shapes to tell their story. Many floor-length dresses, cardigans, coatigans, gilets and scarves were also featured, with comfort at the heart of all garments. A set of four ballet dancers accompanied the models on the runway, reaffirming the timelessness of the pieces.

Scents of Woman, for Spring/Summer 2024, was a colourful and playful display of stripy knits – shorts and tops with matching scarves, long dresses and jumpsuits with a playful spirit. In a fun twist, three dogs appeared on the runway, two of them wearing branded knitted sweaters. In contrast,

Escorpion's collection during Barcelona's 080 Fashion Week 2018 included pieces branded with the logo.

Autumn/Winter 2024, Reconnection, returned to a classic silhouette with knitted dresses in various lengths, shawls and capes in greys and tones of beige, with some garments in berry tones and green – doing what the brand does best. Escorpion is part of Catalan fashion's heritage and produces classic must-have pieces that are timeless and can be handed down through generations.

ANTONIO MIRÓ (1947–2022)

Antonio Miró was one of Barcelona's most accomplished fashion designers. In addition to designing clothes, he also created jewellery, perfume and furniture, and worked in interior design – something he focused on in later years. Albert Villagrasa is now the brand's creative director, a post he has held since 2014.

Born in Sabadell, Miró was advised by his father – a tailor – to work in a textile factory. After this, when he was 19, Antonio decided to open a clothes store with his brother Esteban in Platja d'Aro on the Costa Brava. They called it Groc, meaning "yellow" in Catalan, and the brothers designed and sold garments in the shop, including swimwear, tops, floral men's shirts and trousers.

After two years they closed the shop and moved it to Barcelona's La Rambla, where it began to gather momentum. In 1976, and as a result of its success, Antoni Miró founded his eponymous label. Soon he began to export his collections and was able to show them on international runways in Paris, New York and Tokyo. He also became a regular on runways in Madrid and Barcelona.

A futuristic creation at Antonio Miró's
A/W 2004 collection in Barcelona.

Above: A stunning blue look for Antonio Miró, designed by Alberto Villagrasa, shown during the Barcelona 080 Fashion Week S/S 2017.

Opposite: A play on textures at Antonio Miró's A/W 2005 collection shown at the Passarel·la Gaudí in Barcelona.

Miró won many awards, including the Cristóbal Balenciaga National Fashion Prize in 1988. He was also selected to design the uniforms for the Mossos d'Esquadra, the Catalan police, in 1984, and the outfits for the ceremonies at the Barcelona 1992 Olympic Games. For Barcelona's reconstructed Opera House, the Gran Teatre del Liceu, he designed the curtain, which can be opened from the side as well as vertically.

The designer also enjoyed collaborating with film, television and theatre companies and dressed celebrities including John Malkovich and George Harrison.

But there was another side to him that challenged convention: in 2006, he chose some prisoners to model his collection, and the following year, he selected eight undocumented migrants from Senegal to show his support and highlight their cause.

TOUS

One of Barcelona's most cherished brands, Tous began as a humble jewellery and watchmaker shop. It has become a global leader in affordable luxury and fine jewellery, and manufactures many accessories, including bags, small leather goods, watches, perfume, eyewear and textiles. Since 2012, the company has produced 30 collections every year.

The story began in 1920 when Salvador Tous Blavi became an apprentice watchmaker. By 1930, he moved to Manresa, near Barcelona, and opened a shop with his wife, Teresa Ponsa Mas. Their son Salvador Tous Mas showed such interest in his parents' work that when he was only 12 – in 1953 – he joined his father in the workshop.

In 1965, he married Rosa Oriol, and they took over the shop together. Five years later, Rosa set up a jewellery workshop in the store and began creating her own unique pieces, adding jewellery to the brand's offerings.

In 1985 Rosa also designed their company logo, a teddy bear, inspired by one she saw in a Parisian shop window. This unusual and charming emblem has been cherished by many through generations, and a documentary was made about it, which premiered at the 68th San Sebastián International Film Festival to mark the brand's 100th anniversary. The little bear was also included in the permanent collection in Barcelona's Museu del Disseny (Barcelona Design Museum) in 2017.

"Passion is inevitable when you love what you do."
Rosa Oriol

Tous opened its first store in Barcelona in 1989 in the Bulevard Rosa, which later became the Pedralbes Centre. Throughout the '90s, Salvador and Rosa's four daughters – Rosa, Alba, Laura and Marta – joined the business. It was the start of the brand's global expansion, and soon they opened several stores in Germany, Andorra, Japan and the United States. More shops followed: Mexico in 2001, Puerto Rico in 2003, and Athens, Paris and New York in 2005.

There have been many brand ambassadors for Tous, including Eugenia Martínez de Irujo (Duchess of Montoro), who later designed for the brand, Kylie Minogue and Jennifer Lopez. In 2011 there was a special collaboration with Manolo Blahnik – Manolo Blahnik for TOUS – that produced pendants in gold and silver of his legendary pointed-toe Campari shoe.

SIMORRA

The son of a couturier from Barcelona, Javier Simorra learned the trade and his love of elegant lines from his father. He founded his eponymous womenswear label, SIMORRA, in 1978, and it soon became admired for its attention to detail and for creating beautifully executed quality garments that were made to last.

A new chapter for the brand began in 2016 when SIMORRA and the fabric manufacturer Dimas joined forces. Experts in fabric, the Dimas family added depth to the collections. In 2021, Eva Dimas became head of the brand. She has been working alongside Victoria Mitjans (head of design since 2012) and, collectively, they have rebranded and updated Javier Simorra's legacy.

"Fashion is everything, it is communication. It is art. Fashion is all-encompassing."
Javier Simorra

Together, they create stunning collections that usually begin with a specific material as their initial inspiration and starting point, and focus on traditional techniques and processes to tell their stories. Their Spring/Summer 2024 collection, for instance, was called The Art of Braiding, and was inspired by women, storytelling and the unity of community. They used many intricate weaving techniques to create interesting textures and luxury swimwear in colours that included black, white, natural browns, pale blue, maroon and olive green.

Floral detailing at Javier Simorra's S/S 2007 collection was seen on the runway in Barcelona.

Simorra's finale in 2023, shown at the Mercedes-Benz Fashion Week Madrid, featured contrasting fabrics.

The Memory of Time, their Autumn/Winter 2024 collection, was inspired by fossils and textured fabrics. Many pieces were hand-stitched to create organic patterns and volume, reminiscent of seashells and other organic shapes. The collection featured natural shades like grey, ochre, rust, off-white, green and included jewellery inspired by gemstones.

Their Spring/Summer 2025, The Space Between, was another beautifully executed collection inspired by the Japanese concept of Ma, described as the interval or emptiness in space or the pause in time. This notion was expressed through different techniques. Some garments were layered, such as a denim dress made of thin strips hand-sewn together and woven, creating spaces between them and adding volume and shape. Some were pleated with ribbon. The colour palette for this collection was also organic in its minimalist theme and included many off-white pieces, with some red, soft pink and lime green garments creating a contrast.

Fusing traditional craftsmanship and modern silhouettes is integral to SIMORRA's identity and success, translating into beautiful clothes and collections. There is always a focus on quality fabric, innovation and functional, long-lasting pieces, and at SIMORRA, they embrace both traditional and contemporary concepts simultaneously.

CUSTO BARCELONA

Designer Ángel Custodio Dalmau Salmons, AKA Custo Dalmau, grew up in Barcelona, where he studied architecture. He dropped out to go on a round-the-world motorbike trip with his brother, and was inspired by the relaxed style and vibrant colours of Californian surfer fashion and the psychedelic looks from Northern California.

Street glamour took centre stage at Custo Barcelona during Miami Fashion Week 2018.

"We don't follow trends, but we like to offer unique pieces only."

Custodio Dalmau

In 1980, the brothers founded the brand Custo Line, renamed Custo Barcelona in 1996. Carefree and fun-loving, it has become known for its California-style T-shirts and fun, sexy, colourful graphic garments, which they design for both men and women. They also offer shoes and accessories and have licensed several successful fragrances, including Custo Woman, Custo Man, Pure and Glam Star.

Custo Barcelona has grown and developed a unique style that uses bright colours and geometric shapes in fun collections. Loved by Hollywood, some of the clothes have been featured on *Friends*, MTV, and in films, worn, for example, by Julia Roberts in *Runaway Bride* (1999) and Natalie Portman in *Anywhere But Here* (1999).

Above: A strong and colourful collection from Custo Barcelona was presented at 080 Barcelona Fashion A/W 2024.

Opposite: Julia Roberts wears Custo Barcelona starring opposite Richard Gere in *Runaway Bride*, 1999.

In 2019, Custo Barcelona signed a licensing agreement with the Italian company Velmar (which also makes Moschino's swimwear and lingerie) to produce and distribute their collections worldwide, with Custo Dalmau remaining the brand's creative director. Their first presentation together was a capsule collection for Spring/Summer 2020, unveiled at New York Fashion Week. It was a fun, bright show with many sophisticated minidresses and geometric stripes reminiscent of his architectural knowledge. Shiny fabrics were used in jackets, and there was a nightclub feel to the relaxed but beautifully crafted summery collection. Men's golden swimming trunks and structured swimwear added a '70s feel to the collection.

Custo Barcelona is now participating in Milan Fashion Week, New York Fashion Week and 080 Barcelona Fashion. The company sells in more than 40 countries through over 80 standalone stores and 3,000 retailers across Europe, the USA and Asia.

DESIGUAL

Desigual is a Barcelona-based company that is known for being different, as suggested by its name, meaning "uneven". Twice a year it launches a collection: a Spring/ Summer and an Autumn/Winter, characterized by their colourful prints and unusual designs.

Thomas Meyer, who describes himself as a radical optimist, founded Desigual in Barcelona in 1984. Swiss but born in Germany, Meyer moved to Spain as a child. In 1978, he had two second-hand shops in Barcelona called Babia, and in 1983, he designed his "iconic jacket" made from excess denim stock that he was unable to sell. It was this garment that propelled Desigual's existence. The story goes that he tried to sell it for 20,000 pesetas, and when this didn't work, he sold it in a boutique in Ibiza. The jacket became very popular, and the following year marked the start of Desigual.

The brand's name came from the film-maker Isabel Coixet and had the strapline *No es lo mismo* (*It's not the same*). The first logo was created by the graphic designer Peret and depicted a naked man and woman holding hands. In 1986 Desigual opened its first store.

Desigual was fun and quirky for S/S 2015, as seen during Mercedes-Benz Fashion Week in New York City.

Thomas Meyer moved to Barcelona in 1992 to work on the regular collections. Expansion began when in 2006 Desigual launched a store in Singapore, in New York City in 2009 and in Colombia in 2010.

Some interesting collaborations took place in 2011 with Cirque du Soleil, with whom they developed "Desigual inspired by Cirque du Soleil", and with Christian Lacroix, a collaboration that has been ongoing. They have also collaborated with Disney, including with characters Mickey Mouse and Bambi. One of their most well-known campaigns was for Spring/Summer 2014, which starred Winnie Harlow as their brand ambassador. Their championing of individualism is further apparent in their renewed identity, which included the byline "Love Different".

Today, with a presence in over 107 countries and over 215 stores, Desigual offers collections for women, men and children and has a sports line, as well as accessories and shoes.

"In reality, Desigual isn't a brand. It's a group of people who believe in the power of creativity as a way of life."

Desigual.com

Strong textures and colours added the perfect finishing touch to the Desigual collection shown in New York Fashion Week A/W 2017.

PUIG

Puig is a fashion and beauty conglomerate best known as one of Spain's most established fragrance houses. Founded in 1914 by Antonio Puig Castelló, in 1922 it marketed *Milady*, the first lipstick ever made in Spain. During the 1940s, the company created a cologne called Agua Lavanda Puig, which became one of their hero products and is still a staple in every Spanish household. It was during this time that the company's factory and offices were moved to the centre of Barcelona, near Gràcia, where they had their HQ until 2014.

"We have a unique culture because, throughout our history, we have been guided by a family with sound, firm values that have been passed down from generation to generation."

Puig.com

Antonio's four sons – Antonio, Mariano, José María and Enrique – all joined the business over the years, which allowed for international expansion. Puig collaborated with the designer Paco Rabanne in the 1960s and together they developed the fragrance Calandre. This partnership was so successful that Puig acquired the Paco Rabanne Fashion House in 1987. The '90s were a decade of further expansion: Puig created the fragrances for Carolina Herrera and, in

1995, took over their fashion label; they also worked to create Antonio Banderas Fragrances (1997) and acquired Nina Ricci, which led to a rebranding of their many products to Puig Beauty & Fashion Group. Their fragrance portfolio continued to expand, and in 2002, they took over Comme des Garçons and Prada. It currently also includes Jean Paul Gaultier, Dries Van Noten, Byredo and Charlotte Tilbury.

To celebrate their centenary, their new headquarters near Barcelona, which they called the Torre Puig, was opened in 2014 by Felipe, Prince of Asturias. Ten years later a second adjacent tower, the Torre Puig T2, was unveiled by the same man, now King Felipe VI, and his wife, Queen Letizia of Spain.

Carolina Herrera's CH luxury perfume is part of Puig, a leading player in the beauty business.

chapter 3

ONES TO WATCH

In recent years Barcelona has become one of the most fashionable cities away from the Big Four (Paris, Milan, New York and London). Here are some of the emerging designers shaking things up in the new style capital.

Bielo is a knitwear brand that combines luxury with tradition. Working from his family's atelier in the spectacular setting of La Llacuna, an hour away from Barcelona, Josep Puig Romeu creates delicate pieces that combine Japanese and Catalan designs.

Since the 1980s, the Puig Romeu family has produced luxury knitwear and worked with brands such as Balenciaga, Marni and Givenchy. The brand became well known when the face masks they designed during COVID-19 attracted attention.

“Upon arrival to Bielo, there is a sense of freedom and broad-mindedness; a deceptively simple sentiment, yet highly precious. Just like the collection itself.”

Bielo.cat

Clean silhouettes, here in bright yellow, were present at Bielo's runway presentation during the 080 Barcelona Fashion A/W 2024.

Josep's collections are varied in theme but have a common denominator in their feel and an organic, clean aesthetic. He is very experimental in his approach and has a special lightness about his work. His focus on simplicity is compounded by the use of special techniques when weaving, knitting and pleating, as well as the exclusive use of superior Italian and Japanese yarns.

The brand participates in the 080 Fashion Barcelona runway show, and its Autumn/Winter 2024 collection, The Bather, provides a good example of its ethos. Based on the art of relaxation, the collection reflected the atmosphere of Turkish baths, the colours used by British painter Peter Doig and the Korean art of sea-diving. It championed lightweight knits, intarsia, jacquard, and details such as embroidery and fringing using natural colours – grey and brown combined with shades of ochre, pink, blue and green. Other collections include The Dreamers, The Collectors, The Avantgardes and The Outsiders. When describing their identity, the brand explains, "Underneath Bielo lies a sensuous strangeness. The wilderness of the Catalan mountains mirrors through the brand's aesthetics, its colours and textures."

CARRER

Carrer, meaning "street" in Catalan, is a ready-to-wear fashion label designed by actor Manu Ríos and Marc Forné, his long-term stylist. Ríos is best known for his role in the Netflix Spanish drama *Elite*, where he plays Patrick Blanco, and for starring in Pedro Almodóvar's short film *Strange Way of Life* alongside Ethan Hawke and Pedro Pascal.

Taking inspiration from the founders' favourite cities in the world and drawing from their own wardrobes, the

Marc Forné attends the Loewe Menswear A/W 2023 show as part of Paris Fashion Week, sporting a logo scarf from the brand.

A colourful Gimaguas bucket hat perfectly accessorizes this summery surf outfit in 2019.

"Our design philosophy is 'reworked classics'."

the founders talking to Harper's Bazaar Singapore

urban brand merges street fashion with vintage pieces to create lasting and timeless clothing. When asked who they are designing for, the designers say that their audience is genderless and universal and that they design for everybody. Manu and Marc don't believe in the notion of gender-defining style. They enjoy "gender-bending" by wearing skirts and carrying bags, and wear clothes traditionally designed for men and women. As explained by the designers: "We design for someone who wants to live in style and comfort at the same time, for people who value quality and simplicity, and appreciate the art of being well-dressed, the effortless way."

Their versatile and wearable collections make for clothes that do not follow trends but which are investment pieces. Their utilitarian angle and minimal aesthetic add to a brand that has captured people's attention. Carrer currently offers jackets, trousers, sweatshirts, shirts and overshirts, T-shirts, footwear and caps, all of which are available on their website.

GiMAGUAS

Twin sisters Sayana and Claudia Durany founded Gimaguas (*jimaguas* meaning "twins" in Cuban jargon) in 2018. Sayana studied fashion, while her sister opted to study finance in London. Together, they design beautiful summery garments, including easy-living linen backless

dresses, kaftans and accessories. Their inspiration is global, and their collections often employ artisans worldwide, from Mexico to Madagascar and Jaipur. The brand collaborates with NGOs in Senegal and Nepal to support local crafts and other social projects. As described on the website for Harvey Nichols (one of their UK stockists), "the result is a constant flow of unique items that reflect the brand's love of summertime, travelling and timeless style."

The twin sisters are proud of the fact that all their Gimaguas collections are designed in Barcelona and made in Spain. Their accessories, however, are sourced globally; for example, their gold jewellery comes from India, and their woven hats are from Madagascar.

"When we started to put together what our brand should be, [we thought about] the things we like and what represents us. Some of the words we wrote down were handmade, artisans, unique, adventure, happiness, exotic, barefoot, effortless but chic . . . "

Gimaguas speaking to *Vogue*

PALOMA WOOL

Paloma Lanna (*Lana* means wool in Spanish) founded the independent fashion label Paloma Wool in 2014. Her parents worked in the fashion industry but encouraged her to go to business school rather than fashion college. Her first collection consisted of sweatshirts on which she featured her analogue photography. Each piece was numbered, and a physical picture was sent with every purchase. "I wanted to break the rules, follow my instinct, produce limited timeless pieces and art freely around the act of getting dressed."

Paloma Wool's Womenswear A/W 2023 show was part of Paris Fashion Week.

Paloma's overriding theme has continued to be the exploration of the art of getting dressed, as she explains on her website: "Paloma Wool is my name and the name of this project, which is about getting dressed and the space and ideas that are created around the act of getting dressed."

"The project is based in Barcelona, which has a good, laid-back energy surrounded by nature. You can cross the whole city on your bike, swim in the sea and hike in the mountains all in the same day here."
Paloma Wool

Like many of the emerging Catalan brands, Paloma Wool supports sustainability and a local, limited production, often collaborating with local artists, illustrators and photographers, and projects the awareness and responsibility that comes with selling clothes. She designs for her friends and community and wants to make clothes that will make them feel unique, beautiful and comfortable.

Quiet luxury at Paloma Wool's show during Barcelona 080 Fashion Week S/S 2022.

LEVENS

Mar del Hoyo is a Catalan actress best known for her roles in *Encuentro* (2009), *Crossing Lines* (2013) and *Gallino, the Chicken System* (2012). After a 15-year acting career, she has found a new creative way to express herself by designing and making jewellery. The name "Levens" comes from the place on the French Riviera where she was first inspired to make jewellery.

When she returned to Barcelona from that trip to France, she began to explore diverse ways in which she could create jewellery, using both glass and clay. She attended workshops and classes and turned her own apartment into a workshop. Her creations are not polished and perfect; in fact, she is drawn to the irregularity that the artisan handmade process brings and the meaning it can convey in every piece. And she considers her jewellery to go beyond fashion. Her studio is located on the outskirts of Barcelona, where she lives with her family. Her unique pieces are handmade and, of course, a testament to her dedication to craftsmanship.

"For me, jewellery goes beyond fashion. I see my pieces as small wearable sculptures that accompany you on a daily basis."

Mar del Hoyo

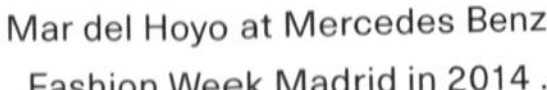

Mar del Hoyo at Mercedes Benz Fashion Week Madrid in 2014 .

chapter 4

STYLE AMBASSADORS

The city of Barcelona provides constant inspiration to visitors and locals alike. There is something for everyone, from delicious food, sports, eclectic fashion, stunning architecture, a vibrant music scene and travel, to name but a few. Some ambassadors of Catalan style and culture channel their creativity online and offer their followers an insight into their personal experiences of life in Barcelona, and their own day-to-day in this beautiful city.

AIDA DOMÈNECH

Aida Domènech began her career in 2009 when she started writing a fashion blog called *Dulceida*. She is also a YouTuber, influencer and businesswoman.

In 2016, she married her girlfriend Alba Paul on the Sitges beach near Barcelona. It was one of the YouTube weddings that received the highest number of views at the time. Her popularity continued to rise, and she was featured in a reality television show that year called *Quiero ser* (*I Want to Be*), where she mentored six fashion influencers alongside Madame de Rosa and Cristo Báñez.

Her book, *Dulceida. Guía de estilo* (*Dulceida. Style guide*), published in 2018, showcases her eclectic style, with added beauty and makeup tips. She has also worked with fashion brands – in 2019 Primark collaborated with her to create a capsule collection called Dulceida X Primark.

In addition to her many roles, Aida Domènech has a business with her mother, Anna Pascual – a talent agency based in Barcelona that represents influencers, called Inmanagement. Aida has also been featured in many fashion magazines and on their covers, notably *Cosmopolitan*. One cover was for *Cosmopolitan Mexico* in June 2020, celebrating Pride.

Angela Rozas Saiz, wearing a NY cap and oversized beige blazer, poses next to Aida Domènech, who is in an oversized button shirt, as they wait outside Alberta Ferretti during Milan Fashion Week – Womenswear A/W 2024.

BLANCA MIRÓ

Described as restless and versatile, Blanca Miró is one of Barcelona's most prominent influencers. A self-confessed fashion lover, she's known for combining unorthodox colours, patterns and style decades, as well as for her eclectic and boho Mediterranean look. A fashion consultant, designer and stylist, she has worked with numerous fashion houses, including Chanel, Dior and Yves Saint Laurent. She is often seen in the front row at Fashion Week. As she herself explains, "I also collaborate with brands with which I feel identified and have a long-term relation. Working with them in different ways from creating content to help them as a stylist or designing a special collection in a specific moment." She also has a huge Instagram following and a separate account where she creates and displays beautiful table settings, a theme inspired by her mother, interior designer Rosarietta Scrimieri.

In 2018, Blanca Miró launched Vasquiat with her business partner, Rafa Blanc. It began as an online platform, but in 2021, a physical store followed: Vasquiat Room, located at Carrer Provença – between the colourful Rambla Catalunya and Barcelona's prestigious Passeig de Gràcia. According to their website, "Vasquiat (pronounced 'vahs-kee-at') is a unique concept store driven by avant-garde fashion and

Opposite: Blanca Miró Scrimieri, Maria de la Orden and Mónica Anoz wear Chanel outfits with Chanel bags outside the Chanel show during Womenswear S/S 2024 as part of Paris Fashion Week.

Overleaf: Blanca Miró Scrimieri wore yellow Roger Vivier pointed heels at "La Maison Vivier" during Paris Fashion Week womenswear A/W 2023.

the community around it. Founded in Barcelona in 2018, we showcase a mix of established and emerging designers carefully curated to bring together style innovation and cutting-edge brands for a community of fashion enthusiasts."

Miró also designs jewellery for Wilhelmina Garcia (a sustainable company that creates handcrafted pieces by artisans in Spain) and is the co-founder and creative director of La Veste (a fun fashion brand specializing in quirky blazers, trousers and hats, launched in 2018 with designer María de la Orden). Blanca is also the co-founder of Delarge – a Barcelona-based sunglasses company launched in 2021. As with the rest of Miro's work, individualism is at the heart of this label – Delarge offers very contemporary designs that are colourful and unusual, using chic geometric shapes (rectangular, circular, hexagonal) in bright colourways, which she designs with Olivia Álvarez.

Blanca Miró married Javi Fondevila in 2022 – the ceremony was held in a dreamlike abandoned castle on the island of Menorca. Her wardrobe for the occasion was extensively reviewed and talked about. She wore a long Loewe patchwork dress for a dinner that took place the night before the wedding, and on the big day, she chose a Dior couture bridal gown from their Autumn/Winter 2018 collection, designed by Maria Grazia Chiuri and created for her by the Dior team in Paris. She wore it with a pair of Loewe's heeled sandals (with a trompe l'oeil crushed egg), natural makeup and her long blonde hair in a simple plait with a hair brooch from her grandmother. She accessorized the outfit with some simple diamond earrings and a ring by Montse Esteve, and for the after-party selected, in contrast, a delightful Paco Rabanne minidress.

La Veste's fun white and orange checked blazer with green and white striped sleeves, as spotted in Paris in 2021.

JESSICA GOICOECHEA

Jessica Goicoechea is a model, influencer and fashion designer who started modelling when she was 15. She has worked for companies such as Rimmel, Calvin Klein and Calzedonia, has been featured in fashion magazines such as *Vogue*, *Glamour* and *Elle*, and has been creating content since 2012.

In 2017, Jessica was in the short movie *La Fantasia*. Her love of fashion and her entrepreneurial spirit took her to found GOI in 2019, a swimwear and ready-to-wear brand that celebrates women's confidence. Her designs have been spotted on Eva Longoria, among other celebrities.

GOI also collaborated with *Playboy* in a sexy and particularly provocative capsule collection in 2024 that included bikinis and figure-hugging dresses featuring the magazine's logo.

LAURA ESCANES

Laura Escanes is a model and influencer who became well known when she dated and married TV presenter and publicist Risto Mejide, who was 22 years her senior, in 2017. Together, they have a daughter, but the relationship ended in 2022.

Escanes featured in the advertising for Majorica, a Majorcan jewellery company, in their 2015 campaign *Why Not?*. The

Jessica Goicoechea wearing a pink and white long coat outside MSGM during Milan Fashion Week Menswear A/W 2020.

Miranda Makaroff at the Desigual X Nathy Peluso collection launch, 2023.

following year, she modelled at 080 Barcelona Fashion and at New York Fashion Week for Custo Barcelona. In 2018, she made her publishing debut with a book of poems, *Piel de letra*, a series of texts that explore her emotions.

MIRANDA MAKAROFF

Miranda Makaroff is the daughter of the Spanish designer Lydia Delgado and Argentine singer Sergio Makaroff. Her rich cultural upbringing has undoubtedly contributed to her many talents: she is an artist, fashion designer, blogger, actress and has also become a much-loved influencer. Miranda has starred in several films, including *A Song for Elaine* (2014), *A la ciutat* (2003) and *Química i prou* (2015).

She is, in addition, a well-respected DJ who has worked for international brands, such as Loewe, Marc Jacobs and Michael Kors. She also DJed at the Golden Globes Awards party for *W* magazine in 2020.

Her career as a fashion designer began in 2011 when she created her first collection, Miranda for Lydia, with her mother Lydia. But Miranda also paints and sculpts and is known for her use of bright colours in her celebration of women and for breaking censorship barriers. Her work was first exhibited in a collective show called *Poder Planetario* alongside the work of artists, including Blanca Miró and Pascal Moscheni. Miranda's art has also been shown at Art Basel Miami Beach, and in art galleries in both Madrid and Ibiza. She designed an artistic installation at the beach-club El Silencio, in 2020, in Ibiza, where she currently lives.

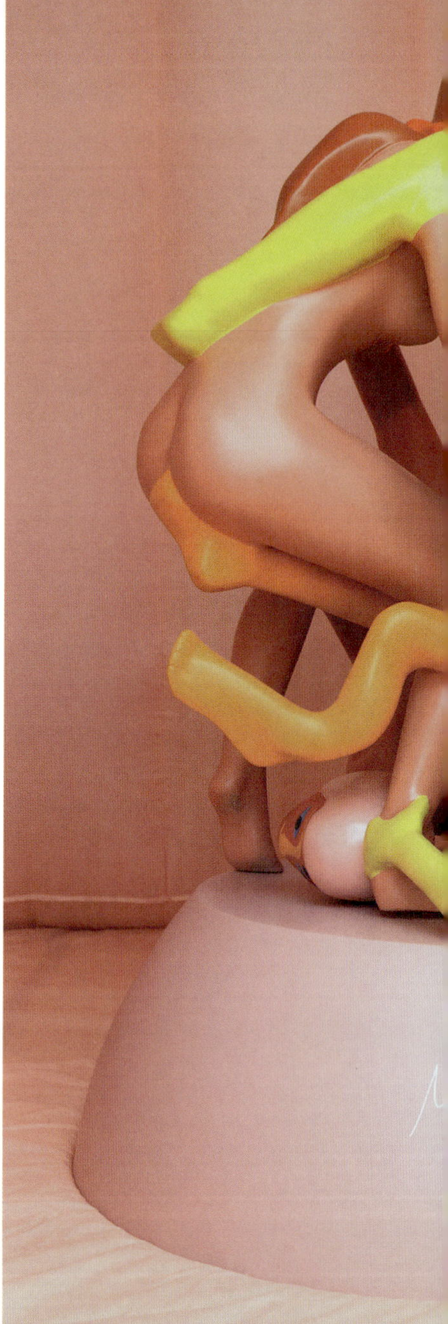

Miranda Makaroff attended the Desigual X Miranda Makaroff sexhibition cocktail party at the Nautilus Hotel during Art Basel Miami Beach 2019.

chapter 5

EVENTS

080 BARCELONA FASHION

080 Barcelona Fashion, also known as Barcelona's Fashion Week, was established in 2007 when it replaced the Passarel.la Gaudí (a runway presentation that ran twice a year in the city between 1984 and 2006, formerly known as Saló Gaudí). The event showcases a mix of talent, ranging from emerging brands to established Catalan and Spanish companies. Above all, it has become a place to display the city's rich legacy.

Barcelona's fashion platform showcases established and emerging talent and strives to shape the industry's future and promote innovation. It highlights critical social issues, raises awareness and creates a dialogue on sustainability, circularity, diversity, ethical fashion and inclusivity.

Away from the fashion weeks for the Big Four (Paris, Milan, New York and London) and alongside similar fashion platforms in cities such as Seoul or Copenhagen, it has become a hub for the local vibrant fashion scene. This prominent fair takes place out of season, in April and at the end of October – a schedule that was originally dictated by the COVID-19 pandemic but which has been kept to reinforce the notion of "out of season" fashion, breaking away from the traditional Spring/Summer and Autumn/Winter framework.

Opposite: Pretty in pink at the Menchén Tomàs fashion show during 080 Barcelona Fashion A/W 2024.

Overleaf: Models walk the runway at the Sita Murt show during Barcelona 080 Fashion Week for S/S 2017.

The 33rd edition of the event introduced 080 Aesthetics, a multidisciplinary space dedicated to digital art and music. Louis Vuitton became an official sponsor for the 34th edition in 2024. Recent event editions have brought together over 20 participants (the 33rd edition of 080 Barcelona Fashion, in 2024, for instance, presented the work of 24 fashion designers), including established names such as Custo Barcelona, SIMORRA and Escorpion and exciting, experimental newcomers such as Dominnico, Outsiders Division, Lola Casademunt by Maite, and Gau. These emerging brands encapsulate the spirit of the city's values and visionary creativity.

The presentation takes place at Barcelona's Modernist complex at the Hospital Sant Pau, designed in 1902 and completed in 1911 by the architect Lluís Domènech i Montaner.

"080 Barcelona Fashion is a fashion platform that promotes the transformation of the fashion sector in Catalonia, both nationally and internationally, through innovation and creativity."

080barcelonafashion.cat

A holiday-inspired collection from TCN showed during Barcelona 080 Fashion Week 2018.

Above: A striking hat was seen at Loa by Lidia Aguilera's show during Barcelona 080 Fashion Week in 2018.

Opposite: Beautiful textures were seen at the Eikō Ai show during Barcelona 080 Fashion Week 2020.

LOUIS VUITTON'S 2025 CRUISE COLLECTION AT THE PARC GÜELL

In 2024, Barcelona's beloved Parc Güell, a UNESCO world heritage site, showcased Louis Vuitton's 2025 Cruise collection. This was a fitting partnership, as the brand is associated with the art of travel.

The precise location was the spectacular Sala Hipòstila (Hypostyle Room), a space with mosaic-tiled ceiling patterns representing the four seasons and the lunar cycles. The space also has a series of 86 imposing Doric-inspired columns, some of which are inclined to create a sense of movement. For the occasion, the room was transformed into a stunning runway with views overlooking the city and the Mediterranean Sea, providing the perfect backdrop to the show.

Nicolas Ghesquière, Louis Vuitton's women's creative director since 2013, paid tribute to the Catalan architect and the city's rich heritage more generally, with a beautiful collection that complemented the setting perfectly and even had a Spanish flavour, most notably with his use of the *cordobés* hat, traditionally made in the southern Spanish city of Córdoba.

The show opened with contemporary tailoring displaying strong shapes that echoed the power-dressing broad-shoulder aesthetic of the 1980s. These looks were accessorized with traditional hats and futuristic-looking mirrored sunglasses. Textures were sensual and experimental, with see-through dresses, intricate lace, ruffles and extraordinary pleated constructions, as well as dotted patterns reminiscent of flamenco costumes and some puffball dresses. There were also some very structured and architectural pieces, with pleating and beading, draping and fringing. Accessories included short boots, some equestrian riding boots and luxurious sculptural earrings. The colour palette was primarily black and white, with a range of earthy tones and grey showing accents of plum, Prussian blue, green and red.

Of course, an A-list audience was present, including actresses Ana de Armas, Jennifer Connelly, Saoirse Ronan, Regina King, Léa Seydoux and Sophie Turner, placing Barcelona firmly on the fashion map.

Above: Louis Vuitton presented the Cruise 2025 collection designed by Nicolas Ghesquière at the Park Güell in Barcelona in 2024.

Overleaf: Barcelona's Park Güell was the perfect venue for the Louis Vuitton Womenswear Cruise 2025 collection.

PRIMAVERA SOUND

This multidisciplinary music festival, known as Primavera (Spring), was founded by Pablo Soler in 2001 as a one-day event at the Poble Espanyol. It has grown exponentially (from selling 7,700 tickets in 2001 to 268,000 tickets in 2024), attracting music lovers globally. Held annually in late May or early June on the waterfront's Parc del Fòrum since 2005, it has become one of the biggest music festivals in Europe. Unlike other similar events which are set on campsites, Primavera is held in the city and provides a stage for long-established bands across many genres (including rock, pop, indie, hip-hop and dance music), encompassing artists such as New Order, The Stooges, Sonic Youth and the Human League, as well as emerging talent. The festival also incorporates exhibitions and installations, adding to the unique experience. This broad range of genres and media means the crowd is hugely varied, as are the unique ensembles worn by attendees – who showcase a broad spectrum of festival chic, from free-spirited bohemian experimental to high fashion.

Primavera started as a one-day event until 2002, when a second day was added, and in 2004, it became a three-day event. A new category called Primavera a la Ciutat (Spring in the City) was incorporated in 2008, with extra shows in several venues across Barcelona. A smaller festival edition, Primavera Weekender, was staged in November 2019 at Benidorm's Magic Robin Hood Camp, a water park with a medieval theme, attended by over 3,500 people.

"Primavera is known for pulling out all the stops when it comes to its lineup, with headliners over the last couple of years including Rosalía, Fred Again, Lana Del Rey, Troye Sivan and Tame Impala, to name a few."

Timeout.com

Dua Lipa performed at Primavera Sound in the Parc del Fòrum in 2022.

After a two-year break due to the COVID-19 pandemic, the 2022 edition lasted two weeks, and then reverted to its usual format. This also celebrated the festival's 20th anniversary. That year, the festival's attendance rose to 460,500 people.

With an impressive, varied line-up of artists, including Pulp, Sonic Youth, Solange, PJ Harvey, Nick Cave and the Bad Seeds, Wu Tang Clan, Blur, New Order, Kendrick Lamar and Rosalía, the festival has become a legendary event in an idyllic setting, with diverse cultural influences and a focus on sustainability. The *New York Times* even dubbed it the Coachella of Europe.

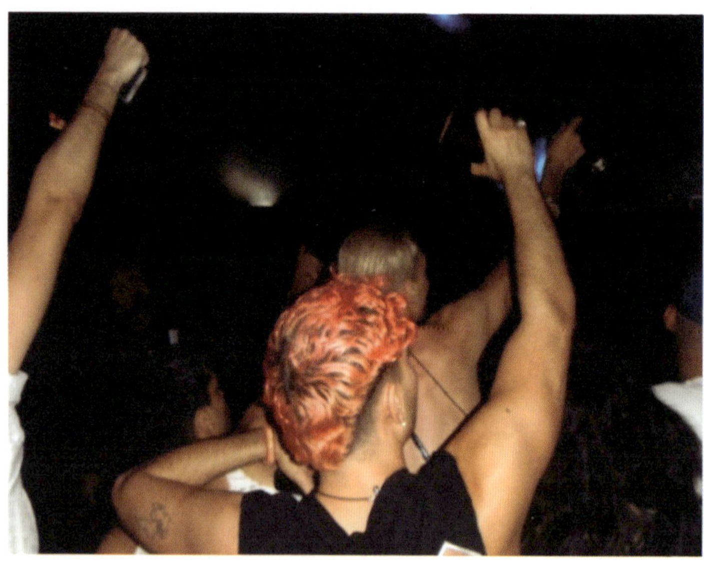

Above: Pink hair and phone lights at Primavera, photographed by Gracie Brackstone.

Opposite: Dressing for the warm days and nights at Primavera, photographed by Gracie Brackstone.

Stylish festival goers enjoy the fabulous weather in Barcelona.

SÓNAR FESTIVAL

This music festival is for fans of techno and electronic beats. Now known as Sónar, the Festival of Advanced Music and Multimedia Art was founded in Barcelona in 1994 by Ricard Robles, Enric Palau and Sergio Caballero.

"A must for anyone wanting to combine the experience of some breathtaking natural beauty alongside a programme of world-leading electronic music."
***Crack* magazine on Sónar Reykjavik**

From the onset, it was divided into two sections, Sónar by Day and Sónar by Night. The festival's first edition took place on 2, 3 and 4 June 1994, at the Centre de Cultura Contemporània de Barcelona (CCCB), where Sónar by Day took place, and at the legendary Sala Apolo, which housed Sónar by Night. This event also had a Record and Technology Fair dedicated to Creativity, a gathering with talks, panel discussions and performances that, since 2013, has become known as Sónar+D and is aimed at industry players. Around 6,000 people attended the launch of this festival.

Spin-off events are organized around the concert, such as OFFSónar, and Sónar has organized events globally – in Bogotá, Buenos Aires, Hong Kong and Reykjavík, among other cities.

The festival's location has changed several times to adapt to its growing needs. In 2013, Sónar Day moved from the CCCB and the MACBA to the *Fira de Barcelona* in Montjuïc, in front of the Plaça d'Espanya. Sónar Night also moved to the Poble Espanyol for a year and then to the Pavelló de la Mar Bella (1997–2000). The headliners for the new venue were Daft Punk. A larger venue, the Fira de Barcelona Gran Via, in L'Hospitalet de Llobregat, has housed the event since 2001.

As the festival has grown, innovation in technology and scenery has become as important as the music itself. In 1998 an online stream was also added, opening it up to a much larger audience, and with a solid audiovisual component, it has attracted performances by artists such as Björk, Kraftwerk and the Chemical Brothers. Despite the big names, the festival has retained its DNA, and kept an open mind by introducing new genres such as reggaeton in 2007, with a performance from the iconic Calle 13.

BRUNCH ELECTRONIK FESTIVAL

Electronik is an open-air nomadic festival that started as a small-scale series of outdoor parties and has grown to take place in Barcelona's Parc del Fòrum, Jardins de Joan Brossa and Nitsa Club, as well as in various cities worldwide. It was created in 2014 as a series of outdoor events.

Brunch Electronik attracts local residents and international revellers alike, creating a fun sense of community among music lovers, DJs and artists. Local bands, emerging artists

“We always wanted to be part of the landscape of the city and we thought the best way to do that was to stick to three key principles: equality, environment, and community.”

Loïc Le Joliff, founding partner of Brunch Electronik

and established international talent are invited to cover many genres, including techno, house, indie and experimental beats.

Brunch is also known for being family-friendly. Many workshops, games and playgrounds are specifically for children, and organizers also work closely with local food providers and chefs, inviting local food trucks to sell their tasty vegan and vegetarian options. “Traditionally, Sundays are days for resting, meeting friends, going to the movies or just relaxing. Still, since last year, Sundays are also Brunch Electronik. Brunch was born last year to become an alternative to traditional Sundays with a versatile program featuring children’s activities, flea markets, vinyl fairs and the performances of the best national and international DJs.”

Brunch Electronik Festival prides itself on being an inclusive event that ensures everybody feels respected and welcome. It adheres to the Barcelona City Council’s protocol *No callem* (*We don’t stay silent*), which addresses male violence. It also has a quiet area in which to unwind. Brunch runs Social Fooding, a foundation that collects unwanted food and distributes it to several NGOs and charities in Barcelona. It is committed to sustainability and aims to be a zero-waste festival.

chapter 6

DRESS LIKE A CATALAN

Stylish white garments, such as this oversized coat, often characterize street style in Barcelona.

SIGNATURE STYLE

Whether you are visiting this cosmopolitan and bohemian city or plan to move there, the local, distinctly chic dress code might inspire you and help you fit right into the Catalan way of life.

The overall Catalan dress code is smart/casual, leaning towards a conservative look. Barcelona, however, is also very forward-thinking, and this is often reflected in the finishing touches that add personality and an eclectic style to the looks. A fun twist is frequently added with accessories, sometimes bold, sometimes colourful, allowing for plenty of individuality, but quality and a good fit are always central to the outfits.

While the seasons determine some of the overall dress codes, the temperate weather allows for many cross-overs, so investing in inter-seasonal outfits is a good idea. And if you want to avoid looking like a tourist in Barcelona, don't wear shorts, vests or swimwear in the city. Instead, opt for a light dress or pair of loose-fitting trousers. Ill-fitting clothes are another no-no, as tailored clothes that are smart and sophisticated are favoured by the locals, especially among older generations, who value quality over quantity. Always looking groomed, the daytime style is mostly relaxed, but Catalans also love to dress up in the evening if going out. They will accessorize most outfits with statement jewellery or a colourful accessory like a scarf or some big, bright bangles.

From shades and great hats to bright-coloured scarves, here is what to wear and what not to wear to blend in and look like a Catalan in style when discovering this magical city.

HERE COMES THE SUN

Being a sunny city most of the year, Catalans always have sunglasses and hats at the ready. Since the main dress code is conservative with a casual twist, classic styles prevail when it comes to sunglasses – you can opt for timeless Ray-Bans (Aviator or Wayfarer), or choose a more modern, coloured frame.

"Barcelona plays an important role in our history as it has witnessed the birth and growth of our company. It's a city open to the world, innovative, rebellious and visionary."

Etnia Barcelona

If you are looking for a local independent eyewear brand, try Etnia Barcelona, a third-generation business founded in the 1950s. As well as their staple sunglasses and colourful eyeglass models, they also create capsule collections and some interesting limited-edition collaborations. These include Casa Batlló × Etnia Barcelona, described by them as a dialogue between modernism, colour and design; FC Barcelona × Etnia Barcelona for the stylish football fans out there; and Primavera Sound × Etnia Barcelona for the ultimate clubbing look. Always striving to be a more sustainable and ethical

Wearing bright colours is part of the city's unofficial summer uniform in Barcelona.

Actress Elke Sommer modelling
woven hats in Barcelona, 1970.

brand, they use natural raw materials and have a social project called the Etnia Barcelona Foundation.

Hats are also worn extensively, especially during the summer months. Choose your preferred look, from wide-brimmed straw sunhats to American-style preppie caps, for a sporty look.

If you are in need of headwear inspiration, head to Sombrerería Mil in the centre of town, a fifth-generation store founded in 1856, which offers its own brand as well as hats from other brands, including Göttmann, Fernandez & Roche and Kangol. There, you can find light Panama and vegetable fibre hats to wear in the summer and warmer felt or wool ones, as well as waterproof styles for winter. You can also purchase a *barretina*, a traditional Catalan hat that is red with black trim and worn primarily on traditional festivals.

SET IT UP

A relaxed city calls for comfortable footwear that can be worn in town and on the beach. When selecting your shoes, there are several styles that the locals wear. Sandals are a good choice in the warmer months. They are usually flat, sporting simple shapes, and made of beautifully crafted leather. But while these are cool and comfortable to wear in the heat, they're not the most practical choice if you plan to walk a lot. Birkenstocks, which have become a universal staple, are another good option that works in the city and may support your feet better than other sandal models.

"Our meeting with Yves Saint Laurent in the 1970s made history in the world of fashion. Together we created the first espadrille with [a] wedge."

Castañer.com

Plimsolls and tennis shoes are a popular choice that the locals often wear across the generations. They are usually made of canvas fabric and available in many colours, making them the ideal shoe for any outfit. Another excellent unisex choice of summer footwear is the espadrille. Typically, a pair will last you the whole season before they start to come apart, and you can walk with them in town as well as on the beach. They now come in every colour and print you can imagine and are breathable and very comfortable.

Above: Crown Princess Leonor of Spain and Princess Sofia of Spain, sporting cool white cotton and wedge espadrilles.

Overleaf: Sunshine, beach and music are key ingredients for a successful festival.

If you are looking for glamorous espadrilles, Castañer is the Catalan go-to brand known for its luxury versions. Founded in 1927 and focused on tradition, craftsmanship and the use of natural materials, the humble shoe was transformed into a sophisticated fashion piece when meeting with Yves Saint Laurent in the 1970s, and the first espadrille wedge was created. Castañer currently manufacture many footwear styles for men and women, but their wedge, in particular, has become synonymous with timelessness and style.

Traditional flip-flops should only be worn on the beach or poolside, and scruffy trainers are mostly reserved for hiking. Winter footwear includes leather boots and stylish trainers.

COTTON CLUB

Unsurprisingly, the warm and dry climate means that the locals favour breathable, natural fabrics such as linen and cotton, especially in the form of shirts, maxi skirts and dresses that can be worn in all seasons. Long skirts and shirts are not only light and comfortable but will also protect you from the sun. Men's shirts, trousers and shorts made of linen will keep you cool and look extremely elegant, and many Catalan men wear them.

Cotton and linen outfits can also be styled to look bohemian, especially when accessorized with baskets, hats, scarves and boho jewellery. In the winter, Catalans opt for thicker fabrics, sweaters and tailored trousers. Jeans, of course, are also a popular choice for this time of year, but they're always chic and on-trend.

COLOUR MATCH

When you're in Barcelona, you might notice that Catalans love to wear accents of colour, reflecting the vibrant city.

Brands such as Custo Barcelona and Desigual, mentioned in Chapter 2, are known for their colourful collections. In the heat, however, lighter pastel colours and a range of natural shades of white are worn to keep the clothing cool, so bright shades are often introduced with the right accessories – sunglasses, a scarf, a belt or some coloured tennis shoes, perhaps. Darker colours are worn mainly in the evening when classic, glamorous outfits fill the city's restaurants, cafés and clubs.

ARM CANDY

Beautiful straw baskets with leather handles are a part of everyday life in Barcelona. Most Catalans own several that can be taken to the market, the beach or carried around the city when off-duty, especially during the summer months.

Some have a zip closure on the top, which is advisable if you are walking around town to keep your possessions safe.

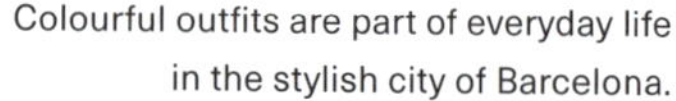

Colourful outfits are part of everyday life in the stylish city of Barcelona.

THE FINE ART OF LAYERING

Layering has become a fine art in a city where the sun shines most of the year. Shawls are a great way to protect your skin from the sun during the day and from the evening breeze. Loose-fitting long-sleeved shirts or cardigans are also very useful, as temperatures can vary significantly from day to night.

You will need a light jacket in spring and autumn, especially in the morning and when the sun goes down, and in winter, you will need a coat– puffa jackets and tailored coats being the most popular – scarves and gloves. You might even need an umbrella, but you should still enjoy plenty of winter sun.

Opposite: Layering clothes is key to adapting to the weather in Barcelona, a stylish way to be ready for any occasion, as seen at the LR3 show during Barcelona 080 Fashion Week S/S 2022.

Overleaf: Blue skies and seas – the view of the city from Park Güell.

INDEX

Page numbers in *italic* refer to photographs

CREDITS

The publishers would like to thank the following sources for their kind permission to reproduce the pictures in this book.

The Advertising Archives: 12

Alamy Stock Photo: Mariano Anton 14; /AP Photo/Joan Mateu 22; /Hervé Donnezan 26; /Emma Durnford 10; / Everett Collection Inc 80; /Lucas Vallecillos 11; /World History Archive 57

Gracie Blackstone: 134, 135, 150-151

Getty Images: Carlos Alvarez 114, 148; /Miquel Benitez 122-123; /Rosie Irene Betancourt/Jeffrey Greenberg/ Universal Images Group via Getty Images 15; /Edward Berthelot 110, 113; /Daniel Boczarski 116-117; /Thomas Concordia 25, 59; /Pablo Cuadra 101, 129, 130-131; /Estrop 60, 65, 66, 71, 81, 83, 90, 97, 98, 121, 125, 154 /Gianni Ferrari/Cover 146; /Lluis Gene/AFP via Getty Images 69; /Juan Naharro Gimenez/Getty Images 76-77; /Dave Hogan 41; /Hulton Archive 18; /Arnold Jerocki/Getty Images for LVMH x Vogue x NBC 45; /Patrick Landmann 8; /Matthew Lloyd/Getty Images for Somerset House 49; /MasterLu 156-157; /Laurie Noble 21; /MN Chan 34; /Mtcurado 30; /Jack Mitchell 42; / John Parra 79; /Cesar RangelL/AFP via Getty Images 70, 75; /Jacopo Raule/ GC Images 93; /Justin Setterfield 52; / Matthew Sperzel 153; /Robert Stiggins/ Express/Hulton Archive/Getty Images 33, 35; /Erik Tanner/WWD/Penske Media via Getty Images 94; /Xavi Torrent 136; /Xavi Torrent/Redferns 7, 46; /Xavi Torrent/WireImage 126, 127; /Dominique Maître/WWD/Penske Media via Getty Images 29; /Raul Urbina/Cover 39; /Jordi Vidal 62-63; / Jordi Vidal/Redferns 133; /Christian Vierig 104, 107, 142, 145; /Christian Vierig/Getty Images for Roger Vivier 108-109; /Victor Virgile/Gamma-Rapho via Getty Images 36, 84

Shutterstock: Irzaza 87